The Spiritual Seasons of Life

by
Evelyn Hamon

foreword by
Dr. Bill Hamon

Christian International Publishers
P.O. Box 9000
Santa Rosa Beach, Florida 32459-9000

Printed in the United States of America

ISBN 0-939868-25-3

Dedication

This book is dedicated to the man who has been my pastor for the last 37 years and whom I married when I was 18 years of age. To my husband, pastor and best friend who has walked with me several times through all the seasons of life.

Appreciation

Appreciation is given to the many individuals who prophesied about the writing of this book and to my friends who kept encouraging me to make these truths available to the people of God.

Special appreciation to Steve Schultz for helping me put these truths into written form.

Foreword

Only a few among the race of human-kind are gifted with the ability to bring wisdom and practical truth to the tragic and triumphant things that we experience in life. Evelyn Hamon was so gifted and has grown and matured in that wisdom over the last four decades. The messages she shares with her audience reveals these great practical truths which help so many people. She does not major on theological, eschatological, or great doctrinal issues, but the real issues of life where the average Christian lives.

The liberating and life giving truths she presents in her messages dealing with such topics as: the spiritual seasons of life, divine flexibility, principles of progress and promotion, and proper attitudes to maintain while one deals with life's challenges and unexpected changes, are the stepping stones for successful living.

Most of the redemptive truths she has learned came from the things she had to live through. Her life challenges and changes came about because of the man she married. When she was 16 years old, a young single 19 year old prophet, straight out of Bible college, began pastoring her home church. Two years later she married her pastor and joined her life to a prophet on whom God had a high calling planned that would require much molding, crushing, remolding and melting down in God's fiery furnace until he perfectly fit in the mold that God had ordained for him.

I can speak authoritatively of all the things she has gone through, for I was instrumental in placing her in most of her life's challenging situations. God seems to take delight in placing two people together who have different backgrounds and opposite personalities. Evelyn's heritage was that of three generations of born again, Spirit-filled and faithful Christians. Her husband was the first among his heritage to become a spirit filled Christian and minister. Evelyn had felt at an early age that she would marry a preacher but she had no personal ambitions other than to be a good wife and mother. Her husband had visions of conquering the world for God and doing more than any other minister had ever done. Evelyn's temperament would have allowed her to be content with living in one area all of her life and to avoid all of life's challenges and drastic changes. But this was not her destiny. God had her marry Bill Hamon not only to help him fulfill his ministry but God had a calling, ministry and destiny for Evelyn to fulfill.

I can honestly say that I know of no other woman who has been so faithful to her man, the ministry and her family. She never once refused to adjust to all the changes we went through: for six years pastoring; to three years of traveling full time evangelistic work with three small children;

to teaching five years in a Bible college; to suddenly and unexpectedly leaving that ministry and being plunged into months of not knowing from day to day what our future would hold; to founding and growing Christian International off-campus College from a vision into 7,000 students world-wide; to founding and growing CI Network of Churches and Prophetic Ministries from one prophet to hundreds of prophets that now circle the globe. Through all these processes of tragic and triumphant changes she has manifested divine flexibility. She has continually worked on her attitude while learning the principles of progress and promotion.

Evelyn's teaching on child raising is backed by the proof of her ministry in raising three children who never once rebelled against God. She trained them in the way they should go and they have never departed from it. Tim, Tom and Sherilyn are now in their 30's, successfully married, in the ministry and have given us 9 beautiful grandchildren who are all serving God and participating in the ministry. All three couples serve on the Christian International Network Board of Governors with their Bishop who is also their Dad. Our life has been successful together in our marriage and ministry. We have continually grown in the 10 "M's" for successful ministry and Christian maturity. Most of this success can be attributed to the stable, consistent, faithful, loving and wise ways of Evelyn, my wife for the last 37 years and co-laborer in the ministry. I jokingly say with all seriousness that the reason men enjoy and relate so much to my wife's teaching is because most of her wisdom and preaching was given to a man, me. I am encouraged that I may have reached some spiritual growth, for now the Lord has released my wife to teach and write books to share these truths with the whole Church.

I can highly recommend this author and the life giving truths she presents. She is for real and the truths she shares are biblically based. May God grant to those who read this book the same biblical soundness, spiritual stability and growth as the author has in the wisdom and ways of God.

Bishop Bill Hamon, ThB.,Th.M.,D.D.
Author: The Eternal Church
    Prophets and Personal Prophecy Vol. 1
    Prophets and the Prophetic Movement Vol. 2
    Prophets, Pitfalls and Principles Vol. 3
Bishop: CI/Network of Prophetic Ministries
President: CI School of Theology, 24 years
Senior Pastor: Christian International Family Church
Prophet: In the corporate Body of Christ

Introduction

As we read and study the N.T. gospels we see that the Lord usually ministered to His disciples and those that followed Him through parables. Jesus used parables to illustrate principles and truths in which many times the objects of His parables were those things which were common to the people of His time.

Likewise, in this booklet, I would like to share with you divine truth which I have learned through life's experiences by using objects and situations which are easy to relate to and common to us in this day and hour. In doing so, I trust that the truth of the four spiritual seasons will bless and refresh you. I pray that it will give you nuggets of divine truth so that it might be stored in your heart for future hope and encouragement.

God has seasons in our lives and a will and a way for us to walk through those seasons. Natural seasons are quite an easy thing for me to relate to since I was raised in the Yakima Valley of Washington state. In this part of the U.S., there are four distinct seasons (unlike tropical climates) and fruit production is a major industry. Looking at God's natural creation teaches us about God's divine nature and ways of working with His children (Rom. 1:20).

Gaining greater understanding and insight into God's *seasonal* dealings will let us realize where we are in relationship to God's seasons and why God has us in a particular season of life. As with anything in life, when we understand the reason for the season and have a vision of the fruit it will produce, we can be at rest and be at peace though we are in the process of growth. We must keep in mind that for those who love God and are called according to His purpose, all things work together for our ultimate good. Some things that happen in our lives are not good but they are designed by God to bring about His overall plan for our life in ministry in Him (Rom. 8:28).

In John 15:1-5, we see Jesus sitting with His disciples at the last supper expounding truth about the Kingdom of God, knowing that His time is very short with His twelve disciples. At this point in the conversation, Jesus parabolically speaks using the natural object of a fruit tree as a picture for tremendous spiritual truth. Here is what Jesus says:

> *"I am the true vine, and my*
> *Father is the husbandman.*
> *Every branch in me that bear-*

1

eth not fruit he taketh away: and every branch that beareth fruit, he purgeth it, that it may bring forth more fruit. Now ye are clean through the word which I have spoken unto you. Abide in me, and I in you. As the branch cannot bear fruit of itself, except it abide in the vine; no more can ye, except ye abide in me. I am the vine ye are the branches: he that abideth in me, and I in him, the same bringeth forth much fruit: for without me ye can do nothing.''

As we read this portion of Scripture, most Christians will identify with and can even quote verse 5, especially the portion that expresses, ''for without me, ye can do nothing.'' However, I would like to call your attention to verse 2 which again states:

2

"Every branch in me that beareth not fruit he taketh away: and every branch that beareth fruit, he purgeth it, that it may bring forth more fruit."

Please note that in this verse, Jesus says that even the branches that bear fruit, even good, tasty, ripe fruit will be purged. Since we are the branches, God states in this parable that even when we are doing the best we can, trying our hardest to be a good Christian and making an effort to reach our full potential, the Father still purges us! He doesn't cast us away, He just purges us so that we might bring forth **more** fruit.

In order to impart the truth of this Scripture, I would like you to think of yourself as a peach tree, grape vine or some type of tree that produces fruit. We are now going to talk about the divine will and way of God's seasons in your life as a fruit tree (branch) which God has created to produce

3

much fruit for His Kingdom. As Ecclesiastes states:

> *"To every thing **there is a season,** and a time to every purpose under heaven:" Ecc. 3:1*

So, let us go on to the first season of life.....

THE SPRING SEASON

In the spring season of your life, you have been born again and have been planted into the Body of Christ like a small seedling who has been raised in an agricultural hot house. Spiritually speaking, the seed of God's word has been implanted within your heart and you have started to grow in the Holy Spirit's "seedling nursery."

Within this hot house environment, you have been secure and protected from life's harsher elements. You are potentially a great fruit tree but at this stage you look more like a stick in the ground with a couple of barren branches. As funny as this stage of development might seem, all trees go through an initial growth spurt where they are skinny, have no leaves, and even look like they are a dead stick. Of course, the little tree knows that it's not dead and that it has grown a long way from the little seed from which it started.

About this time, the farmer arrives at the nursery looking for small trees from which to build his new orchard. He then gathers the new seedlings together and takes them to his field and begins to plant them within the orchard. As the farmer sets each tree in the ground, he waters and fertilizes it so the roots are stabilized and so that the seedling will be established and thrust into a new growth time.

The spiritual counterpart to this period is when you, as a believer, begin to find yourself and your particular place in the

Lord. You begin to attend foundational believer's classes and with an insatiable hunger, you begin to devour the Word of God with great intensity. The Word of God and the Spirit of God are like natural water and fertilizer to your inner soul. Oh it feels *sooooo good!* It is spring time; the sun is warm, the soil is rich, the rains are frequent, it's beautiful outside, and the farmer is taking such good care of you. It is a time when you have come a little way in the Lord and are beginning to feel comfortable in your Christian walk. You are making new friends and even the pastor of the church notices you and thinks that you can be developed into something. The leadership recognizes your potential and begins to put a lot of input into your life. Possibly you have even gone through some in-depth counseling so that you can begin to become everything the Lord has called you to be.

All totalled, this time of life can be summed up by one word — *growth*. That's what all young seedlings seem to do in the spring time. Grow, grow, grow! Every day that the farmer goes out to check the orchard, he'll see new development on the seedlings: a new limb here, a new bud there. The new seedling is growing up and filling out and soon, before you know it, there are new leaves appearing on the little branches. It actually appears to be alive! It looks so cute and pretty out in the orchard and the farmer is taking such good care of the little fruit tree.

This is "spring." This season is causing the little tree to come into fruition and prompting it to grow at a rapid pace. In this season you, like the tree, are being blessed! You are not being reproved very much. You are just taking in all the good things of the Lord. Everyone seems like an angel and is there continually to encourage and help. It is a time of growing many leaves and branches which are helping you to continue to absorb the benefits of the "Son."

7

Of course, the next season of life to evolve is......

THE SUMMER SEASON

Truths

At the beginning of summer season, you are like one of God's young trees in His orchard. You have been establishing many branches and displaying a full crown of colorful leaves. Now something new begins to appear — **new little buds!** Do you know how exciting these little buds are to young little trees?!? You, as a little tree, have never had buds before and all of a sudden you have **buds.** Seeing these buds gives you such a sensation of growth, a new experience with joy and a sensation that new and wonderful things are continually happening.

Revelation

The spiritual counterpart to this time is when you at last begin to be used in some capacity by the Lord. Finally you can work in the nursery or possibly you have been

8

given a new position in the Sunday school area or maybe you have been given a position in the ladies ministry or even used ushering. Regardless of the position, you finally feel like you are somebody! You are a tree with some buds!

As the summer progresses the buds begin to enlarge and you start to wonder, *"What in the world is going on?" "What are these new things?"* As time advances your buds eventually evolve into full grown blossoms. As a young tree, you have finally received the radiant "fragrance of the Lord" and everyone that comes by hugs you and conveys to you that, *"You are so great and you are such a blessing to be around!"* You are really beginning to feel like you have developed into something great in God because you have blossoms all over your tree. You smell so good and look *sooooo pretty*. When you come to church everyone notices that you have arrived because you have such a sweet fragrance and a radiant smile. It is a time in life when you are receiving a lot of sunshine and a lot of rain. Everyone seems to be encouraging and blessing you. You are so excited because you might have even stepped out recently and given your testimony in church and someone was blessed by it! You are growing so fast in God. You hardly know what to do with yourself!

All of a sudden, the little blossoms begin to wither away and fall off. You do not feel like you can do quite the things you were doing. For a while you begin to think, *"What is going on?" "Am I backsliding?"* At this time you begin to back up on a few things, evaluate and search yourself closely.

One day, during this evaluation process, you notice that under the little peach blossoms there are small little peaches. **Yes!** Little tiny baby fruit. Once again you become excited because you come face to face with the reality that you are really producing

10

something that can bless the people of God. You begin to feel a sense of anticipation and fulfillment because you see something growing in your life that will demonstrate to others God's ultimate plan for all believers — that of producing good fruit for others.

As the summer season slowly passes, your fruit continues to grow. Your tree looks vibrant and healthy with its full load of maturing fruit and shiny green leaves. At this time you might have a cell group in your home or possibly you are being used as head over a department in the church. God's blessings are continuing to overtake you. People are picking your fruit on a continual basis. You are giving fruit here and there. It feels so wonderful that you hope this season will last forever. You are seeing people being blessed. Possibly you have even prayed for the sick and been used of the Lord in the area of the fruit of faith with healings and miracles.

11

During this summer season, you might experience and weather a few storms that cause a little discomfort but like all summer storms, they come and go and don't last very long.

I remember one "spring and summer season" in our lives which began in 1964. We had been through three years of a winter season, when spring time began with the call from a Bible college for my husband to come and teach. We had just experienced a hard winter season so when we knew it was time to plow and get ready to plant our seed again, it was exciting. During our time of preparation to go and become a part of that ministry, it was hard to be patient and let our tree grow leaves and blossoms again. Finally, preparation was complete and we went to begin five years of very fruitful ministry. We were able to minister and give our fruit to many young people who are in ministry even today. It was a time of fulfillment and blessing in our lives. Oh, we had

12

storms but most of the time was spent giving away our fruit. We didn't have any great pressure or responsibility during this time.

As summer season progresses and as people are drawing fruit from your life, you come to the realization that no more new fruit is coming up out of you. Even if this is your first summer as a small tree and you did not produce a great quantity of fruit, to you it seemed like a lot! Maybe even the quality of the fruit was not that choice but again, to you it seemed pretty good! Let's face it. God the Father is happy that you produced fruit and likewise the pastor is happy to see you producing something usable within the local church family.

Eventually the day arrives when someone or something comes along and picks your last piece of fruit! At this same time you notice a change in the environment and realize you are beginning to enter into another new spiritual season of life which is......

THE FALL SEASON

This little peach tree has never been through the four seasons of spring, summer, fall and winter. Since he left the hot house he has only experienced spring and summer, and has assumed that this is the way it is always going to be. He is about to enter into two more seasons that will seem to contradict everything that has happened to him thus far. What he is about to go through will not make any sense to him until summer season comes again. At that time, he will see the benefits of bigger and better fruit in his life and ministry because of what happened during the fall and winter season.

As the tree enters the fall season the winds begin to blow a little harder and the temperature begins to drop. As a tree, you have given away all of your fruit and you might not understand why God has not replenished all the lovely produce you have given away. You begin to feel a little strange because you have been used by the Lord to bless the people. During the summer you have given great congregational prophecies, helped to lead worship, been used of the Lord in gifts of healings. But now you are beginning to feel empty.

Again you begin to face another time of self-evaluation. You analyze yourself and begin to ask yourself questions such as, *"Have I lost my first love?"* or *"Am I losing my zeal for God?"* You find yourself not rejoicing as much in church services or possibly even sitting further toward the back of the church. In times past you always sat on the front row, were the first to volunteer and always said "AMEN" the loudest.

You begin to say to the Lord, *"If these are the results of growing up in God, then I don't want to grow up!"* You can stomp your feet, lay on the ground and even confess all you want, but the fall season will still come. (Believe me, I have tried to evade it myself! I have used every resource at my disposal to make it pass by! Yet, it still comes!)

Now keep in mind that through the past seasons you have produced many leaves, buds, blossoms and great succulent fruit but now the fruit is gone, the blossoms are gone and the buds are gone. The only thing you have left to show and display are your pretty green leaves.

All of a sudden, as the cold winds begin to blow, your leaves change color and begin to fall off! Your heart begins to cry out, *"Oh no, this is the only thing I have left to display!"* But it is to no avail because very soon all your leaves are on the ground and you are standing there with bare, naked branches.

Oh, things look awful dismal but you adjust your attitude and look at some of the remaining positives. Praise God, you are still in the orchard. Praise God, you still have all your branches. Praise God, the sunshine comes out some of the time. You say, *"I don't feel as good as I used to but I'll just get in there and plug away. Maybe I'm overworked or this is burn-out or I'm just tired."*

The sap of your strength begins to leave your branches and it begins to return to the trunk of the tree and roots. You just don't seem to have the energy that you once had because, like the tree, you are entering a stage of dormancy, otherwise known as.....

THE WINTER SEASON

Winter season is a tough period for everyone and everything, including trees. It is so cold! (And I really detest cold weather!) It is a season when you can step outside and take a deep breath and feel like your own lungs have frozen. You bundle up in so much clothing that you can hardly move! Yes, winter has arrived and it happens to all of us.

In the winter season of life, the coldness of life makes you numb and you don't feel God's presence anywhere. Your branches are hanging bare, frozen solid, and there is snow all over your trunk. Possibly the only time you sense God's presence is when you read and study the Word of God. But what you don't realize is that you are growing underground because you are growing in faith. You are not producing fruit above ground, but underground you are growing a greater root system of faithfulness, patience, longsuffering, endurance, hope and steadfastness.

Your roots are getting bigger, spreading out and going deeper which is causing you to become stronger and more stable in God. When the winds of adversity blow against you, you are not uprooted because your root system in God is deep and extensive. Jesus does not want you to be the type of Christian that has no depth in your root system which would cause you to wither away the moment persecution arises. Matthew 13:20 states:

> *"But he that received the seed into stony places, the same is he that heareth the word, and anon with joy receiveth it; Yet* **hath he not root in himself,** *but endureth for a while: for when* **tribulation** *or* **persecution** *ariseth because of the word, by and by he is offended."*

God is always working with us. He is either doing a work through us to others or a greater work deep within our spirit-root system. If it were up to us, we would want to produce fruit year round and never think about our roots. But God has a way of ex-

19

tending our spiritual roots so that we can become more stable and stronger in Him. God knows that we, as spiritual trees, are going to grow bigger branches and greater fruit so we must have an adequate root system to support and provide nourishment for the above-ground growth we will experience in the next spring season of life.

During the winter time, we must realize that there is not much we can do about this season. It will come into the life of every committed Christian. Like the fall season, we can fuss, kick and complain, but it will still come. For God has ordained it for our best interest. As the Apostle stated in 2 Corinthians 4: 15-17:

> *"For all things are for your sakes, that the abundant grace might through the thanskgiving of many redound to the glory of God. For which cause we faint not; but though our*

outward man perish, yet the inward man is renewed day by day. For our light affliction, which is but for a moment, worketh for us a far more exceeding and eternal weight of glory;"

PERSONAL ILLUSTRATIONS

Please allow me to share some personal examples of this season. In times past, my husband, Bill, used to travel extensively without me. During the first 15 years of our marriage, we spent much of our time together in ministry. But then a time came when the Lord began to speak to me about my husband having to travel without me. For about a year I kept having these thoughts and impressions and I rebuked them frequently. In typical Christian fashion I kept saying, *"Get thee behind me satan! I married my pastor. I have been with him in ministry. We were set up in ministry to be together. I am not supposed to be alone."*

And on and on and on I went. I had it down pat! But do you know what? It did not change God's mind at all! God had decided that I was going to stay home, watch the children and I was going to grow there while my husband was traveling in ministry without me. Yes, **God knows where you are going to grow the most and He allows these things in your life.**

During this period, I gave God, my children, and my husband a hard time. Quite honestly, I was not being good (today my children will verify this!). When my husband would call on the phone from across the country, without realizing what I was doing, I would put a guilt trip on him by saying such things as: *"This isn't God, because you should be home with your children! This can't be God because God wouldn't want this!"* Then I would hang up the phone and

22

run to the bedroom and cry. Yes, during one of my long winter seasons I really did that!

Do you think God brought my husband back home? No! God was not intimidated by me. He knew my heart. He would say to me, *"Evelyn, straighten up. Adjust your attitude. This is winter time and you are going to grow through this."* I came to the realization through this process that you cannot threaten God! Some people try their best to coerce God through threats. They say to God, *"I can't take any more of this. God, if you don't change my situation and circumstances I'll go back to my old ways and get drunk or start smoking again...."*

God used this time to teach me to trust Him more and to have some confidence in myself. I had always been very dependent on my husband. Now, I not only had to make decisions about my family, but also take some of the responsibilities for Christian International Ministries.

Praise God that He never changes! He looks upon us in this winter season and says, *"If that is what you have to do, then I won't stop you. But I'm not going to stop my winter season just because you don't like it. I love you too much to see you go your own way."*

I learned some of God's ways during those Winter Season years. But it was about 10 years later during the time of our son's wedding (Tom's) that I came to a more mature understanding of God's purpose for His four seasons in the lives of His chosen ones.

Some of our friends and relatives were preparing to travel to Little Rock, Arkansas to attend the wedding of our youngest son and future daughter-in-law, Tom and Jane. At the time, we were living in Arizona and all 14 of us loaded up in a van and a mini-motor home and headed east. Bill and

I were in the second vehicle, the van, while part of the family was leading the way in the mini-motor home. When we arrived in Oklahoma City, we pulled over for breakfast, ate and then loaded back up for the remainder of the trip. Before we took off again, we all prayed for a continued safe trip. The mini-motor home pulled onto the freeway first and we followed within a few minutes.

We had advanced only about a mile down the road when we came upon an accident. As we neared the accident sight, we suddenly realized that it was our mini-motor home! It had turned over on its top, slid 187 feet down the highway, and then burst into flames. Nine of my immediate family were in this particular vehicle (My mother; my sister Donna, her husband Leon Walters, and three daughters; my sister Marilyn and her two daughters). We instantly ran up and began to pull people out of the wrecked burning vehicle.

There was my family, lying on the side of the road, burned and cut. It was terrible! We kept looking for my little 6 year old niece, Crystal (Marilyn's daughter), who had been visiting us for the past two weeks and was to be in the wedding. But we shockingly discovered that she was trapped under the motor home and there was no way to get her out. All our efforts failed and through our tears and heartache, God chose to take her home.

Yes, I felt like God had totally deserted me. That is exactly what you feel like in winter! (I'm not telling you this to make you sad but to say that winter seasons do come but thank God, they do come to pass!)

We stayed in Oklahoma City late into the night making sure that my mother and Donna's daughter (Devra), who were both badly burned, received hospitalization. Then Bill, some of the family and I continued to Little Rock for the wedding. We were very excited about Tom and Jane's wedding, but very sad about our niece's death. It was hard to reconcile our emotions. We had our son's wedding on Saturday and then on Sunday we drove to East Texas where Bill conducted the funeral of our niece on Monday.

From there, we left Texas and went to Pensacola, Florida for some meetings. While in route, I felt emotionally wrung out. We arrived at night. The next morning we pulled back the curtains and were shocked by the view that greeted us — we were located right next to a cemetery! Can you imagine that? (To this day, we have never seen another motel that overlooks a graveyard!)

While we were there, I would jump every time the phone rang. I would immediately think it was bad news about the family who were still in the hospital. I was definitely in a state of emotional dilemma! One moment I would feel good about staying with Bill and the next, I would feel guilty about not staying in Oklahoma City with the family. It was a hard place to be because I realized that staying with Bill in Pensacola was not a neccesity, but I also knew that I had no place to stay in Oklahoma City. My mother was terribly burned and lingering between life and death but my sister and her husband were there with her and her daughter. It seemed like our whole world was falling apart and the devil was doing everything he could to destroy us.

While at the meetings in Pensacola, God's grace was great because people would come up to us after the meetings and tell us how blessed they were by our ministry. My husband preached several times during those five days and personally prophesied to over 200 people. Quite honestly, neither I nor my husband hardly remember those five days of meetings because of the great emotional turmoil we were experiencing.

When the meetings were over, we decided to go about 70 miles to our daughter and son-in-law's place in Defuniak Springs, Florida for a short visit. All the way there I was saying to God, *"You know God that I cannot take any more! This is the limit of my endurance! I have had it! This is too much and I can't handle any more! I feel like I have been skinned alive and every nerve is exposed. I can't take one thing more!"* Like all of us, I felt like I needed to inform God of my horrible situation! I kept saying, *"This winter is too tough! The snow is too deep and I can't even see my bottom branches! I don't want anything else in my life! Do you hear me God? I can't take one thing more."*

The next day while at Glenn and Sherilyn's place, Bill and Glenn decided to go for a dune-buggy ride. Then the most incredible thing happened — Bill flipped the buggy over and broke his arm! It was no small fracture because we had to rush him to a hospital 45 miles away for immediate surgery.

We were all sitting in the waiting room of the hospital and I was quite anxious to find out about Bill's condition. Glenn volunteered to go find out what was happening in surgery, which left me alone. During this time, God began to speak to me. He said, *"I thought you said you couldn't take any more?"* And I said, *"I did!"* He then said, *"Well, how are you handling this and what are you going to do about it?"*

I was in such a serious state of mind at that time, that I truly reviewed all the options open to me. I thought about leaving Bill and all the family. I contemplated getting drunk. (Which is quite a thought since I have been raised in a Christian home and don't know anything about drinking! I wouldn't even know what to ask for if I entered a bar!) I thought about having a nervous breakdown but I realized that a nervous breakdown does not last forever

and eventually I would have to come back
and face the reality of life. (That option
seemed to be a new trial in itself!) Last, going insane had no appeal to me.

Yes, I thought about all the options including becoming angry with God but that
is all I did — I just thought about it. Finally I said, *"God, You know, there is nothing else but You. No matter how deep the
winter is, You are the only one I have."* God
*spoke to me and said, "Now, don't you ever
tell me again what you cannot take because
I am the only One who really knows how
much you can take."*

I felt like Moses when he stood before
the Lord and tried to convince God that he
couldn't talk. Like Moses, God knew me
better than I knew myself. He knew how
much I could take. I stood through it all
and I have become much stronger because
of it. In this particular winter season, a
peace came into my spirit because of my

31

willingness to confront the situation with God.

Through this winter season of calamity and traumatic happenings, God delivered me from any fear of future happenings and gave me a divine confidence that I can make it through whatever the future may hold.

In looking back on this eventful time in our lives, my husband and I realized God's plan in all of this for our lives. (Sometimes you have to wait and look back.) In that two week time in June of 1981, we had gone back and forth from *hot* to *cold* emotionally many times — Getting ready and traveling to our son's wedding (hot); the accident along the way (cold); Saturday the wedding (hot); on Monday the funeral (very cold); Tuesday through Sunday night meetings in Pensacola (hot); the next Tuesday Bill breaks his arm and is in the hospital 5 days (cold); then on Sunday we left Florida to go to Oklahoma for Bill's parents

50th wedding anniversary (hot); then we finally go home to Arizona. Thank God that winter season ended and spring came again!

Looking back we realized that God had used this time to test us to see if we were trustworthy and stable enough for the greater ministry and purpose He had planned for our life and ministry. We were like the **steel rails on the railroad** which go through the extreme temperature change testing to see if they will withstand bending, breaking, cracking or warping. Only then will they trust the rail to carry the train with its people and cargo.

So God took us through those extreme hot and cold emotional times to see if we would hold straight and not bend, crack, break, or warp before He entrusted us with the great responsibility of being pioneers in the *Prophetic Movement*. If we had not passed the tests and gone through the winter season with the proper Biblical attitude,

33

then God would have had to use someone else to fulfill His purpose in the Prophetic. After we came through that winter season with the right attitude and spirit, God began to set in motion all things necessary to bring about the great world-wide ministry we are responsible for today.

The Lord is so good. We can get so deep in the snow but eventually the snow begins to melt down and things begin to look a little brighter. Like my experience in Oklahoma City and in Florida, we sit in the orchard and tell the farmer, *"I can't take any more. I can't take any more of this."* But what does the farmer do during or at the end of winter? HE PRUNES YOU!

The purpose of winter is to bring the tree into a place of dormancy and inactivity so that the tree can be purged by pruning. Pruning cannot be done in the summer time when the sap is flowing out into the branches of the tree in abundance. It is the mercy and wisdom of the farmer that causes him to wait until winter season before pruning the tree.

In winter all you have left to your life is these little bare limbs. You've lost all your leaves and have endured the bitter cold. About the time you see relief in sight, the farmer (the Lord) comes along and lops off your last remaining branches. He says, *"You have too many limbs and My Word says that those who bear fruit are the ones whom I purge."*

Yes, when you are at your worst time — all the anointing is below the surface of feeling and emotion, you don't feel God anywhere, He has seemingly given you more than you can handle — then He comes and says, *"Alright, I'll let up on the cold but now I am going to prune you!"* He then begins to prune away all those things that we have worked so hard to grow. But it must happen at this time. If the Lord pruned us during the summer, all of our sap would run out and we would die.

Have you ever watched anyone prune a tree? A big tree becomes a bunch of little stubby limbs. All those great limbs that produced such marvelous fruit are being cut off! To the natural mind, it seems ridiculous because the old limbs were not bad. They had produced good results! But some of the limbs we grew are in conflict with others. Some of our attitudes and actions that grew during our fruitful ministry season were extreme and had to be cut back to God's standard. Those who are spiritually minded realize that if God let the branches remain, then we would begin to trust more in our branches than we do in God. We would begin to rely more on our own ability to produce, than in God's ability to produce through us.

Yes, He prunes us so that we can grow new branches which are bigger and better.

As the seasons pass and as we mature, our fruit becomes larger and more delicious. We come to realize that unless a tree is pruned, it cannot produce a greater quantity and better quality of fruit. A tree left to itself becomes a snarled mess! It has live and dead branches growing everywhere and the fruit becomes little, bitter, and sour. You couldn't even give the fruit away because no one would want it. But when the tree is pruned back and allowed to grow, it then produces more. Pruning the limbs back allows them to grow bigger and stronger. If the limbs are allowed to grow long and thin, then when a big crop is grown on them, the weight causes the limbs to split off from the tree thus hindering the fruit from reaching harvest.

When we allow God the same opportunity to plant us, fertilize us, and to prune us, then the spring season comes around again. This time our branches have been pruned symmetrically and we develop into a larger tree that is more organized and balanced with a greater capability of producing bigger and better fruit.

Every year the farmer does this to his trees. This process of the four seasons and the pruning in the winter eventually brings forth the greatness and majesty of the trees with their beautiful prize winning fruit. Please understand that regardless of the season, the tree is in the will of the farmer as long as it stays rooted and grounded in the orchard. We, like the trees, can be in God's perfect will even when the circumstances around us look very dismal and bleak.

Last, realize that some winters are easier than others even though each has a pruning time. You might pass through three winters that are mild but eventually you'll come to a hard cold freeze that does a deeper work. During these times, if you don't feel condemned in your spirit and you don't feel guilty before God because of sin in your life, then you are probably just in a winter season. However, if you do feel convicted, then you need to reevaluate, repent and get out of the wintry storm of disobedience as fast as possible!

IN CLOSING

Thank God for all the seasons! He created them for a purpose. When we realize that He has ordained these seasons, then the seasons of life will work in our favor. We can come to realize that there is a time and a season for every purpose under heaven and thereby we can learn to be content with God's processes in our lives. As Habakkuk 3:17-19 states:

> *"Although the fig tree shall not blossom, neither shall fruit be in the vines; the labour of the olive shall fail, and the fields shall yield no meat; the flock*

39

> *shall be cut off from the fold,*
> *and there shall be no herd in*
> *the stalls: Yet I will rejoice in*
> *the Lord, I will joy in the God*
> *of my salvation. The Lord*
> *God is my strength, and he will*
> *make my feet like hinds' feet,*
> *and he will make me to walk*
> *upon mine high places.''*

We should note that in this process of spiritual seasons, there are three seasons of the year that are life giving, joyfully progressive and fruitful. There is only one winter season that is filled with cold, miserable days which seem to bring about restriction, regression and loss. This shows us that most of our seasons of life should be times of progressive growth, joyful living and productive ministry.

As I shared earlier, the summer of 1981 was a tremendously hard winter season for us. But not long after this hard winter season we moved our ministry and staff to North Florida where we entered into a fresh spring season of plowing and planting. Since then, we have been in a summer time of growth and fruit production for the last six years. Oh yes, we have had a few storms but they were summer storms that soon passed. Praise God! He is faithful to always be consistent and cause blessing to come into our lives if we remain in His will and don't give up.

May this truth set you free by bringing the revelation of God's ways of making us into seasoned, mature Christlike Christians.

Mature Christians are those who have gone through enough of God's seasons until they understand His ways. They are not moved to discouragement or despair by their circumstances. Like Apostle Paul, they have lived long enough and gone through enough to discover that when you are a committed child of God, you love Christ with all your heart and are called according to His own purpose — then you **know** by revelation and experience the biblical truth that: *"all things are for your sakes"* *"If God be for us then who can be against us."* For God makes *"all things work together for our good."* So we *"rejoice evermore and in all things give thanks."* For nothing or no one can separate us from God's blessings and purpose for our lives. Let us rejoice in all seasons whether spring, summer, fall or winter. They are all ordained of God for our ultimate good and fruitfulness in Christ Jesus. Remember, it is those who victoriously go through the seasons of life who become seasoned and matured Christians.

If we will allow God to take us through the four seasons — the ups and downs, the hot and the cold times — then we, like the steel railroad tracks, will be strong enough to receive and carry God's greater blessings. Allow the seasons to do their work in and through your life so that you will hear Him say, "Well done thou good and 'fruitful' servant, enter into the joy of the Lord. You have been faithful in these few areas, now I will double your joy, anointing, ministry and productivity in My Kingdom."

Fulfilling Your Personal Prophecy

Pastors, make sure all of your leadership and members have their own copy of this vital booklet.

Everyone who thinks they have received a personal word from God needs this booklet.

Buy in quantity and give one to each person who receives a Personal Prophecy through your ministry.

SPECIAL VOLUME DISCOUNTS

Number of Copies	Price Per Copy	Approximate % Discount
1	$3.95	
2 to 10	$2.96	25% Discount
11 to 99	$2.40	40% Discount

IF YOU BUY A FULL CASE OF FULFILLING YOUR PERSOANL PROPHECY YOU MAY RECEIVE A 60% DISCOUNT.

Evelyn Hamon's
Newest Release

• • • • • • • • • •

Evelyn reveals life giving truths essential to being a victorious overcomer. Discover how God's test are His proving grounds for promoting, perfecting and prospering us. Biblical stories and personal life experiences are shared with the reader. If you have gone through some trials and tests that didn't seem to be positive to you this book will reveal truth that will set you free. You will be able to live with greater peace and joy after reading this book..

$3.95

Please refer to the resource page in the back of the book, to order your personal copies of Evelyn's books and tapes.

Evelyn Hamon's
Books and Tapes
• • • • • • • • •

In this book, **Evelyn,** gives a practical, natural look at the spiritual storms of our lives. She brings an uplifting and encouraging message that will help you to succeed in weathering life's changes.

$3.95

In this tape series, **Evelyn,** shares wisdom and insight on the principles of progress & promotion, divine flexibility, spiritual seasons, and maintaining a positive attitude. **$20.00** (Four 60 minute tapes)

In this tape series, **Evelyn,** offers encouragement and practical application for growing through the stages of God, determination in destiny, family life in ministry, and husband & wife relationships. **$20.00** (Four 90 minute tapes)

Please refer to the resource page in the back of the book, to order your personal copies of Evelyn's books and tapes.

Dr. Bill Hamon's
Latest Cassette Tapes Sets

· · · · · · · · · ·

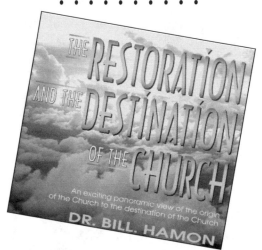

The Restoration and the Destination of the Church

· · · · · · · · · ·

A heavenly satellite overall view of the Church from its origination to its ultimate destination. The greatest information available on the progressive restoration of the Church unto its end time ministry and eternal destiny. The history and future of the Church from a Prophet's view.

$50.00 (Ten 90 minute tapes)

The Coming Saints' Movement

. . . .

What's next for the Church? Essential insights concerning the next restorational move of God. A must for those who want to be a part of God's last moves. Revelation of God's purpose for the Saints' Movement and what it will accomplish in the Church and the world. (Two 90 minute tapes)

$10.00

Principles to Live By

. . . .

Bishop Bill Hamon presents six major Biblical principles that have helped him fulfill 50 years of successful Christian living and 47 years of ministry.
(Six 90 minute tapes) **$30.00**

Please refer to the resource page in the back of the book, to order your personal copies of Dr. Hamon's books and tapes.

The 10 M's

• • • • • • • • • •

This powerful series was developed to help you mature in and maintain your ministry. This series investigates 10 major areas of our personal lives which we need to continually examine and correct if we are to prove ourselves to be true ministers of God. **$15.00** (Three 90 minute tapes)

Prophetic Pitfalls

• • • • • • • • • •

This exciting tape series is an in-depth look at the pitfalls that face today's Christians. Dr. Hamon uses biblical characters to disclose the subtle satanic pitfalls which can cause leadership and saints to fall.

$35.00 (Seven 90 minute tapes)

Plugging Into Your Spiritual Gifts

• • • • • • • • • •

CI's finest ministers in an array of teaching on the gifts of the Holy Spirit. This tape series will bring encouragement and build up your faith to manifest the gifts God has placed within you. **30.00** (Six 90 minute tapes)

Please refer to the resource page in the back of the book, to order your personal copies of Dr. Hamon's books and tapes.

Jane Hamon's

The Deborah Company

Dreams and Visions

• • • •

Jane Hamon gives us an understanding of the seemingly hidden messages of our dreams and visions. It's time we learn to discern the voice of the Lord as He communicates His mind, heart, purpose and plan to us through the language of dreams and visions. This is the most biblical and balanced presentation written by a proven Christian Prophetess.

$10.00

God is releasing keys of revelation and spiritual principles that will unlock the latent potential of power on the Church and bring strategic breakthrough in these important days. Women will have a unique part to play in this last days army that God is assembling. The time is at hand in which God is activating the gifts which have been deposited by His Spirit into every blood-bought, Spirit-filled believer, regardless of gender. It is a day for women to step out from under their cloaks of inactivity and step into their God-ordained identities as active, vibrant members of the Body of Christ. **$10.00**

Please refer to the resource page in the back of the book, to order your personal copy of Jane Hamon's book.